Byron

Passionate Romantic

First published in Great Britain by Brockhampton Press,
a member of the Hodder Headline Group,
20 Bloomsbury Street, London WC1B 3QA

ISBN 1 86019 308 0

Created and produced by Flame Tree Publishing,
part of The Foundry Creative Media Company Limited,
The Long House, Antrobus Road, Chiswick, London W4 5HY

Special thanks to
Kate Brown and Kelley Doak for their work on this series

Printed and bound in U.A.E.

Byron
Passionate Romantic

Written and Compiled by
O. B. DUANE

BROCKHAMPTON PRESS

Contents

Introduction

Although he exerted a powerful influence on Romanticism, Byron's individual genius stemmed from the fact that he did not aspire to intense spirituality or philosophical pretension in his work. 'I always write best when truth inspires me,' he once commented, and unlike many of his contemporaries, repeatedly sacrificed the value of words to the sincere expression of the fruits of his experience. As famous for his scandalous personality as his poetry, Byron's popularity and public worship reached an extraordinary height during his lifetime, still unrivalled by any other poet.

George Gordon Byron was born in London, the son of Captain Byron, who enjoyed a brief career in the Guards, and Catherine Gordon, a young heiress from Scotland. Also known as 'Mad Jack', Byron's father was a disreputable character and after he had been disinherited by his own father, spent his time pursuing wealthy, society women. His first successful conquest was the Marchioness of Carmarthen who left her husband to elope with him, allowing 'Mad Jack' access to her £4000 a year fortune. A daughter, Augusta, who was later to play a crucial role in the poet's life, was the only surviving child of this marriage.

When the Marchioness died in 1784, Captain Byron sought another rich and innocent victim and after only a two-month courtship married the twenty-year-old Catherine Gordon in the spring of 1785. Within a short time, however, the young heiress's fortune had been squandered and by the time Byron was a year old, the family were forced to move to Aberdeen to escape a string of creditors. The marriage now in financial ruin, 'Mad Jack' abandoned his wife and retreated to France where he died in 1791 at the age of thirty-six.

Byron spent his early childhood in relative poverty in Aberdeen under the watchful eye of his mother, whose behaviour towards him alternated between displays of intense affection and uncontrolled outbursts of rage. His life was made even more miserable by the fact that he had been born with a deformed right foot, a defect he could never quite come to terms with, even later on in adult life.

At the age of ten, Byron unexpectedly succeeded to the barony following the death of his great-uncle. He now left Scotland for Nottinghamshire to assume his new role and settled with his mother in the dilapidated ancestral home of Newstead Abbey. In the Spring of 1801, he was sent to Harrow public school where he proved himself a clever student and an enthusiastic reader, albeit reluctant to devote himself seriously to his studies. He maintained this idle attitude when he went up to Cambridge in October 1805 and began to exercise a rare talent for drawing attention to himself. Before long, he had established his reputation as a 'hot youth', renowned for his debauched, rakish behaviour. During his second year at Cambridge he still continued to neglect his studies, but devoted at least a proportion of his time and energy to the task of printing and distributing his first collection of poems.

Fugitive Pieces, circulated privately in November 1806, contained some of the very first verses Byron had ever written, centring on a theme of unrequited love and closely imitating the earliest, sentimental lyrics of Thomas Moore. In the summer of 1807, Byron issued an expanded edition for widespread publication and named the collection *Hours of Idleness*.

Byron's juvenilia met with a disparaging reception. An article in the *Edinburgh Review* harshly dismissed his poems as little more than 'stagnant water'. Although deeply offended by this and similar rebukes, Byron refused to abandon poetry but turned his talents instead to vindicating his literary reputation. Almost immediately, he began writing a long satire in the manner of his great idol, Alexander Pope, entitled *English Bards and Scotch Reviewers*. Published in March 1809, the poem constituted a vicious attack on his critics, as well as a highly satirical appraisal of popularly approved poets, among them Wordsworth, Southey, Scott and Coleridge.

Shortly after his satire appeared, the young Byron took his seat in the House of Lords and then set off on a two-year tour of Europe, visiting Spain, Malta, Portugal and Greece. During this time abroad, he gathered together much of the material he was to use in *Childe Harold* and as soon as he returned to England began preparing the first two cantos for publication. Hailed as the greatest poem of modern times when it appeared in March 1812, the impact of *Childe Harold* on Byron's life is best described in the poet's own simple words: 'I awoke one morning and found myself famous.' At twenty-three, Byron became an overnight celebrity and was flattered and praised wherever he went. His cavalier personality and handsome features aroused a universal curiosity, but he held a particular fascination for the women he encountered, many of whom energetically competed for his amorous attentions.

During the intervening four years before he began the concluding cantos of *Childe Harold*, Byron wrote many of his finest longer poems, including *The Corsair*, *The Giaour* and *Ode to Napoleon Buonaparte*, and he also completed the collection *Hebrew Melodies*. He thoroughly enjoyed living in a glare of publicity and it was at this time that he embarked upon a number of complicated love-affairs, including his notorious affair with Lady Caroline Lamb. In 1815, he married Annabella Milbanke, but the marriage was a disaster from the outset, since London society had already turned against the young poet, prompted by the rumour that he was carrying on an incestuous affair with his half-sister, Augusta Leigh.

In the spring of 1816, a deeply embittered and socially ostracized Byron departed England, never to return. Yet he was fiercely determined to triumph over misfortune, and during a four-month stay in Geneva, began writing the poetic drama *Manfred*, the third canto of *Childe Harold* and *The Prisoner of Chillon*. He moved from Geneva to Venice in November and spent the majority of his time here during the next three years, revelling in the city's lively, hospitable atmosphere. The fourth canto of *Childe Harold*, inspired by a lengthy visit to Rome, was finished in early 1817, at which point Byron was determined to depart from his old melancholic style in favour of a more ironic, humorous approach to his writing. *Beppo*, which appeared in 1818, was intended to 'repel the charge of monotony and mannerism' which Byron felt had become his trademark, and was written in a deliberately colloquial, anecdotal style which he again returned to in his last great work, *Don Juan*.

By the autumn of 1818, Byron had completed the first canto of *Don Juan*. Determined to challenge the insular prejudices of contemporary English poets, he showed no restraint in mocking the solemn epic, producing a 'real life' poem, steeped in sharp wit and ironic detachment. The story of the first Canto, describing the sexual antics of the sixteen-year-old Don Juan, provided ample material for critics to declare the verses both 'filthy and impious' when they were first published in London in 1819. Shelley, however, applauded their 'stamp of originality' and 'defiance of imitation', while Goethe expressed great admiration for the poem and encouraged Byron to continue the work.

Between 1819 and 1823, while Byron lived with the woman he described as his 'last love', Countess Teresa Guiccioli, he remained highly prolific, completing another fifteen cantos of *Don Juan*, as well several dramas and long poems, including *Marino Faliero*, *Cain*, *Heaven and Earth* and *The Vision of Judgement*. Through the Countess' family, he became actively involved in politics once more and lent his support to Italian patriots seeking to challenge Austrian-backed Papal authority. By 1823, he had found a new outlet for his political interests and turned his attention towards Greece, a country he had fallen in love with when he visited it in his youth. Ever since that time, he had supported the idea of Greek independence from the Ottoman Empire and now began to feel strongly that action was more important than words.

Byron had told his friend Lady Blessington, 'I have a presentiment I shall die in Greece. I hope it may be in action, for that would be a good finish to a very *triste* existence.' In January 1824, he arrived in Missolonghi, but he had not yet seen any action when he contracted fever. Within two months he was dead, leaving unfinished his masterpiece, *Don Juan*.

Author's Note

This selection of Byron's poems, chosen from across his short, yet incredibly productive career, attempts to give an overview of the poet's vast catalogue of work, from his most popular shorter lyrics, to his longer epic poems. It has only been possible here to reproduce extracts from Byron's longer works, which include *Childe Harold* and *Don Juan*.

Chronology

1788 George Gordon Byron, sixth Lord Byron, is born on 22 January to John Byron and Catherine Gordon.

1798 At the age of ten, he succeeds to the family title and moves with his mother to Newstead Abbey, in Nottinghamshire.

1800 He is enrolled at Harrow School.

1805 He attends Trinity College, Cambridge University.

1807 His first volume of verse, *Hours of Idleness*, is published and is bitterly attacked by critics.

1809 Byron publishes his Popean satire *English Bards and Scotch Reviewers* and departs England for an extended tour of Europe.

1811 He returns to England and takes up residence in London.

1812 The first two cantos of *Childe Harold* are published, bringing him overnight success.

1813 Several long poems, including *The Giaour*, *The Bride of Abydos* and *The Corsair* are published. His anguished affair with Lady Caroline Lamb is now at its height.

1814 *Ode to Napoleon Buonaparte* and *Lara* are published. Byron proposes to Annabella Milbanke for the second time and is accepted.

1815 He marries Miss Milbanke in January and their daughter Ada is born the following December. *Hebrew Melodies* is published.

1816 Byron's wife decides to separate from him and returns to her parents' home. An embittered Byron leaves England permanently in April, eventually settling in Venice. Canto III of *Childe Harold* and *The Prisoner of Chillon* are published.

1817 His mistress Claire Clairmont, bears him a daughter,

Allegra. *The Lament of Tasso* and *Manfred* are published.

1818 Canto IV of *Childe Harold* and *Beppo* are published. Byron begins work on his epic masterpiece, *Don Juan*.

1819 *Mazeppa* and the first two cantos of *Don Juan* are published anonymously.

1820 Byron lives in Ravenna with his last love, Countess Teresa Guiccioli. *The Prophesy of Dante* is published.

1821 Cantos III, IV and V of *Don Juan* are completed. Byron also writes several dramas, including *The Two Foscari*, *Sardanapalus*, and *Cain*.

1823 He finishes Cantos VI-XIV of *Don Juan* and leaves Genoa for Greece to join Greek insurgents against the Turks.

1824 He dies at Missolonghi of fever on April 19. The Deans of Westminster Abbey and St Paul's refuse him a burial and he is finally laid to rest at Hucknall Torkard, close to the family home of Newstead.

On Leaving Newstead Abbey

'Why dost thou build the hall, son of the winged days? Thou lookest from thy tower to-day: yet a few years, and the blast of the desert comes, it howls in thy empty court.' – Ossian

THROUGH THY battlements, Newstead, the
hollow winds whistle;
Thou, the hall of my fathers, art
gone to decay;
In thy once smiling garden, the
hemlock and thistle
Have choked up the rose which late
bloom'd in the way.

Of the mail-cover'd Barons, who
proudly to battle
Led their vassals from Europe
to Palestine's plain,
The escutcheon and shield, which
with every blast rattle,
Are the only sad vestiges
now that remain.

No more doth old Robert, with
harp-stringing numbers,
Raise a flame in the breast for
the war-laurell'd wreath;
Near Askalon's towers, John
of Horistan slumbers,
Unnerved is the hand of his
minstrel by death.

Paul and Hubert, too, sleep in
the valley of Cressy;
For the safety of Edward and
England they fell:
My fathers! the tears of your
country redress ye;
How you fought, how you died, still
her annals can tell.

On Marston, with Rupert, 'gainst
traitors contending,
Four brothers enrich'd with their
blood the bleak field;
For the rights of a monarch
their country defending,
Till death their attachment
to royalty seal'd.

Shades of heroes, farewell!
your descendant,departing
From the seat of his ancestors,
bids you adieu!
Abroad, or at home, your
remembrance imparting
New courage, he'll think upon
glory and you.

Though a tear dim his eye at
this sad separation,
'Tis nature, not fear, that
excites his regret;
Far distant he goes, with
the same emulation,
The fame of his fathers he
ne'er can forget.

That fame, and that memory, still
will he cherish;
He vows that he ne'er will
disgrace your renown:
Like you will he live, or like
you will he perish;
When decay'd may he mingle his
dust with your own!

If Sometimes in the Haunts of Men

IF SOMETIMES in the haunts of men
Thine image from my breast may fade,
The lonely hour presents again
The semblance of thy gentle shade:
And now that sad and silent hour
Thus much of thee can still restore,
And sorrow unobserved may pour
The plaint she dare not speak before.

Oh, pardon that in crowds awhile
I waste one thought I owe to thee,
And, self-condemn'd, appear to smile,
Unfaithful to thy memory:
Nor deem that memory less dear,
That then I seem not to repine;
I would not fools should overhear
One sigh that should be wholly *thine*.

If not the goblet pass unquaff'd,
It is not drain'd to banish care;
The cup must hold a deadlier draught,
That brings a Lethe for despair.
And could Oblivion set my soul
From all her troubled visions free,
I'd dash to earth the sweetest bowl
That drown'd a single thought of thee.

For wert thou vanish'd from my mind,
Where could my vacant bosom turn?
And who would then remain behind
To honour thine abandon'd Urn?
No, no – it is my sorrow's pride
That last dear duty to fulfil:
Though all the world forget beside,
'Tis meet that I remember still.

For well I know, that such had been
Thy gentle care for him, who now
Unmourn'd shall quit this mortal scene,
Where none regarded him, but thou:
And, oh! I feel in *that* was given
A blessing never meant for me;
Thou wert too like a dream of Heaven
For earthly Love to merit thee.

The First Kiss of Love

AWAY WITH your fictions of flimsy romance;
Those tissues of falsehood which folly has wove!
Give me the mild beam of the soul-breathing glance,
Or the rapture which dwells on the first kiss of love.

Ye rhymers, whose bosoms with phantasy glow,
Whose pastoral passions are made for the grove;
From what blest inspiration your sonnets would flow,
Could you ever have tasted the first kiss of love!

If Apollo should e'er his assistance refuse,
Or the Nine be disposed from your service to rove,
Invoke them no more, bid adieu to the muse,
And try the effect of the first kiss of love.

I hate you, ye cold compositions of art!
Though prudes may condemn me, and bigots reprove,
I court the effusions that spring from the heart,
Which throbs with delight to the first kiss of love.

Your shepherds, your flocks, those fantastical themes,
Perhaps may amuse, yet they never can move:
Arcadia displays but a region of dreams:
What are visions like these to the first kiss of love?

Oh! cease to affirm that man, since his birth,
From Adam till now, has with wretchedness strove,
Some portion of paradise still is on earth,
And Eden revives in the first kiss of love.

When age chills the blood, when our pleasures are past –
For years fleet away with the wings of the dove –
The dearest remembrance will still be the last,
Our sweetest memorial the first kiss of love.

When We Two Parted

WHEN WE two parted
In silence and tears,
Half broken-hearted
To sever for years,
Pale grew thy cheek and cold,
Colder thy kiss;
Truly that hour foretold
Sorrow to this.

The dew of the morning
Sunk chill on my brow –
It felt like the warning
Of what I feel now.
Thy vows are all broken,
And light is thy fame;
I hear thy name spoken,
And share in its shame.

They name thee before me,
A knell to mine ear;
A shudder comes o'er me –
Why wert thou so dear?
They know not I knew thee,
Who knew thee too well: –
Long, long shall I rue thee,
Too deeply to tell.

In secret we met –
In silence I grieve,
That thy heart could forget,
Thy spirit deceive.
If I should meet thee
After long years,
How should I greet thee?
With silence and tears.

Maid of Athens, Ere We Part

Ζώη μοῦ, σᾶς ἀγαπῶ.

MAID of Athens, ere we part,
Give, oh, give me back my heart!
Or, since that has left my breast,
Keep it now, and take the rest!
Hear my vow before I go,
Ζώη μοῦ, σᾶς ἀγαπῶ.

By those tresses unconfined,
Wooed by each Aegean wind;
By those lids whose jetty fringe
Kiss thy soft cheeks' blooming tinge;
By those wild eyes like the roe,
Ζώη μοῦ, σᾶς ἀγαπῶ.

By that lip I long to taste;
By that zone-encircled waist;
By all the token-flowers that tell
What words can never speak so well;
By love's alternate joy and woe,
Ζώη μοῦ, σᾶς ἀγαπῶ.

Maid of Athens! I am gone:
Think of me, sweet! when alone.
Though I fly to Istambol,
Athens holds my heart and soul:
Can I cease to love thee? No!
Ζώη μοῦ, σᾶς ἀγαπῶ.

Fare Thee Well

'Alas! they had been friends in youth;
But whispering tongues can poison truth;
And constancy lives in realms above;
And life is thorny; and youth is vain;
And to be wroth with one we love,
Doth work like madness in the brain;

But never either found another
To free the hollow heart from paining –
They stood aloof, the scars remaining,
Like cliffs, which had been rent asunder;
A dreary sea now flows between,
but neither heat, nor frost, nor thunder,
Shall wholly do away, I ween,
The marks of that which once hath been.'
COLERIDGE'S CHRISTABEL

FARE THEE well! and if for ever,
Still for ever, fare thee well:
Even though unforgiving, never
'Gainst thee shall my heart rebel.

Would that breast were bared before thee
Where thy head so oft hath lain.
While that placid sleep came o'er thee
Which thou ne'er canst know again:

Would that breast, by thee glanced over,
Every inmost thought could show!
Then thou wouldst at last discover
'Twas not well to spurn it so.

Though the world for this commend thee –
Though it smile upon the blow,
Even its praises must offend thee,
Founded on another's woe:

Though my many faults defaced me,
Could no other arm be found,
Than the one which once embraced me,
To inflict a cureless wound?

Yet, oh yet, thyself deceive not;
Love may sink by slow decay,
But by sudden wrench, believe not
Hearts can thus be torn away:

Still thine own its life retaineth,
Still must mine, though bleeding, beat;
And the undying thought which paineth
Is – that we no more may meet.

These are words of deeper sorrow
Than the wail above the dead;
Both shall live, but every morrow
Wake us from a widow'd bed.

And when thou wouldst solace gather,
When our child's first accents flow,
Wilt thou teach her to say 'Father!'
Though his care she must forego?

When her little hand shall press thee,
When her lip to thine is press'd,
Think of him whose prayer shall bless thee
Think of him thy love had bless'd!

Should her lineaments resemble
Those thou never more mayst see,
Then thy heart will softly tremble
With a pulse yet true to me.

All my faults perchance thou knowest,
All my madness none can know;
All my hopes, where'er thou goest,
Wither, yet with thee they go.

Every feeling hath been shaken;
Pride, which not a world could bow,
Bows to thee – by thee forsaken,
Even my soul forsakes me now:

But 'tis done – all words are idle –
Words from me are vainer still;
But the thoughts we cannot bridle
Force their way without the will.

Fare thee well! thus disunited,
Torn from every nearer tie,
Sear'd in heart, and lone, and blighted,
More than this I scarce can die.

Lines to a Lady Weeping

WEEP, DAUGHTER of a royal line,
A Sire's disgrace, a realm's decay;
Ah! happy if each tear of thine
Could wash a father's fault away!

Weep – for thy tears are Virtue's tears –
Auspicious to these suffering isles;
And be each drop in future years
Repaid thee by thy people's smiles!

And Thou Art Dead, As Young and Fair

AND THOU art dead, as young and fair
As aught of mortal birth;
And form so soft, and charms so rare,
Too soon return'd to Earth!
Though earth received them in her bed
And o'er the spot the crowd may tread
In carelessness or mirth,
There is an eye which could not brook
A moment on that grave to look.

I will not ask where thou liest low,
Nor gaze upon the spot;
There flowers or weeds at will may grow,
So I behold them not:
It is enough for me to prove
That what I loved, and long must love,
Like common earth can rot;
To me there needs no stone to tell,
'Tis Nothing that I loved so well.

Yet did I love thee to the last
As fervently as thou,
Who didst not change through all the past,
And canst not alter now.
The love where Death has set his seal,
Nor age can chill, nor rival steal,
Nor falsehood disavow:
And, what were worse, thou canst not see
Or wrong, or change, or fault in me.

The better days of life were ours;
The worst can be but mine:
The sun that cheers, the storm that lowers,
Shall never more be thine.
The silence of that dreamless sleep
I envy now too much to weep;
Nor need I to repine,
That all those charms have pass'd away
I might have watch'd through long decay.

The flower in ripen'd bloom unmatch'd
Must fall the earliest prey;
Though by no hand untimely snatch'd,
The leaves must drop away:
And yet it were a greater grief
To watch it withering, leaf by leaf,
Than see it pluck'd to-day;
Since earthly eye but ill can bear
To trace the change to foul from fair.

I know not if I could have borne
To see thy beauties fade;
The night that follow'd such a morn
Had worn a deeper shade:
Thy day without a cloud hath pass'd,
And thou wert lovely to the last;
Extinguish'd, not decay'd;
As stars that shoot along the sky
Shine brightest as they fall from high.

As once I wept, if I could weep,
My tears might well be shed,
To think I was not near to keep
One vigil o'er thy bed;
To gaze, how fondly! on thy face,
To hold thee in a faint embrace,
Uphold thy drooping head;
And show that love, however vain
Nor thou nor I can feel again.

Yet how much less it were to gain
Though thou hast left me free,
The loveliest things that still remain,
Than thus remember thee!
The all of thine that cannot die
Through dark and dread Eternity
Returns again to me,
And more thy buried love endears
Than aught except its living years.

Stanzas for Music

THEY SAY that Hope is happiness;
But genuine Love must prize the past,
And Memory wakes the thoughts that bless:
They rose the first – they set the last;

And all that Memory loves the most
Was once our only Hope to be,
And all that Hope adored and lost
Hath melted into Memory.

Alas! it is delusion all:
The future cheats us from afar,
Nor can we be what we recall,
Nor dare we think on what we are.

So, We'll Go No More A Roving

I

SO, WE'LL go no more a roving
So late into the night,
Though the heart be still as loving,
And the moon be still as bright.

II

For the sword outwears its sheath,
And the soul wears out the breast,
And the heart must pause to breathe,
And love itself have rest.

III

Though the night was made for loving,
And the day returns too soon,
Yet we'll go no more a roving
By the light of the moon.

To Thomas Moore

I

MY BOAT is on the shore,
And my bark is on the sea;
But, before I go, Tom Moore,
Here's a double health to thee!

II

Here's a sigh to those who love me,
And a smile to those who hate;
And, whatever sky's above me,
Here's a heart for every fate.

III

Though the ocean roar around me,
Yet it still shall bear me on;
Though a desert should surround me,
It hath springs that may be won.

IV

Were't the last drop in the well,
As I gasp'd upon the brink,
Ere my fainting spirit fell,
'Tis to thee that I would drink.

V

With that water, as this wine,
The libation I would pour
Should be – peace with thine and mine,
And a health to thee, Tom Moore.

Oh! Weep for Those

I

OH! WEEP for those that wept
by Babel's stream,
Whose shrines are desolate, whose
land a dream;
Weep for the harp of Judah's
broken shell;
Mourn – where their God hath dwelt
the godless dwell!

II

And where shall Israel lave
her bleeding feet?
And when shall Zion's songs
again seem sweet?
And Judah's melody once
more rejoice
The hearts that leap'd before
its heavenly voice?

III

Tribes of the wandering foot
and weary breast,
How shall ye flee away
and be at rest!
The wild-dove hath her nest,
the fox his cave,
Mankind their country –
Israel but the grave!

She Walks in Beauty

I

SHE WALKS in beauty, like the night
Of cloudless climes and starry skies;
And all that's best of dark and bright
Meet in her aspect and her eyes:
Thus mellow'd to that tender light
Which heaven to gaudy day denies.

II

One shade the more, one ray the less,
Had half impair'd the nameless grace
Which waves in every raven tress,
Or softly lightens o'er her face;
Where thoughts serenely sweet express
How pure, how dear their dwelling-place.

III

And on that cheek, and o'er that brow,
So soft, so calm, yet eloquent,
The smiles that win, the tints that glow,
But tell of days in goodness spent,
A mind at peace with all below,
A heart whose love is innocent!

On This Day I Complete My Thirty-Sixth Year

Missolonghi, Jan. 22, 1824.

'TIS TIME this heart should be unmoved,
Since others it hath ceased to move:
Yet, though I cannot be beloved,
Still let me love!

My days are in the yellow leaf;
The flowers and fruits of love are gone;
The worm, the canker, and the grief
Are mine alone!

The fire that on my bosom preys
Is lone as some volcanic isle;
No torch is kindled at its blaze –
A funeral pile.

The hope, the fear, the jealous care,
The exalted portion of the pain
And power of love, I cannot share,
But wear the chain.

But 'tis not *thus* – and 'tis not *here* –
Such thoughts should shake my soul, nor *now*,
Where glory decks the hero's bier,
Or binds his brow.

The sword, the banner, and the field,
Glory and Greece, around me see!
The Spartan, borne upon his shield,
Was not more free.

Awake! (not Greece – she *is* awake!)
Awake, my spirit! Think through *whom*
Thy life-blood tracks its parent lake,
And then strike home!

Tread those reviving passions down,
Unworthy manhood! – unto thee
Indifferent should the smile or frown
Of beauty be.

If thou regrett'st thy youth, *why live?*
The land of honourable death
Is here: – up to the field, and give
Away thy breath!

Seek out – less often sought than found –
A soldier's grave, for thee the best;
Then look around, and choose thy ground,
And take thy rest.

The Vision of Judgment

EXTRACT

I

SAINT PETER sat by the celestial gate:
His keys were rusty, and the lock was dull,
So little trouble had been given of late;
Not that the place by any means was full,
But since the Gallic era 'eighty-eight'
The devils had ta'en a longer, stronger pull,
And 'a pull altogether,' as they say
At sea – which drew most souls another way.

II

The angels all were singing out of tune,
And hoarse with having little else to do,
Excepting to wind up the sun and moon,
Or curb a runaway young star or two,
Or wild colt of a comet, which too soon
Broke out a bounds o'er th' ethereal blue,
Splitting some planet with its playful tail
As boats are sometimes by a wanton whale.

III

The guardian seraphs had retired on high,
Finding their charges past all care below;
Terrestrial business fill'd nought in the sky
Save the recording angel's black bureau;
Who found, indeed, the facts to multiply with such
rapidity of vice and woe,
That he had stripp'd off both his wings in quills,
And yet was in arrear of human ills.

The Destruction of Sennacherib

I

THE ASSYRIAN came down like the
wolf on the fold,
And his cohorts were gleaming in
purple and gold;
And the sheen of their spears was
like stars on the sea,
When the blue wave rolls
nightly on deep Galilee.

II

Like the leaves of the forest when
Summer is green,
That host with their banners at
sunset were seen:
Like the leaves of the forest when
Autumn hath blown,
That host on the morrow lay
wither'd and strown.

III

For the Angel of Death spread his
wings on the blast,
And breathed in the face of the
foe as he pass'd;
And the eyes of the sleepers wax'd
deadly and chill,
And their hearts but once heaved,
and for ever grew still!

IV

And there lay the steed with his
nostril all wide,
But through it there roll'd not the
breath of his pride;
And the foam of his gasping lay
white on the turf,
And cold as the spray of the
rock-beating surf.

V

And there lay the rider
distorted and pale,
With the dew on his brow, and
the rust on his mail:
And the tents were all silent,
the banners alone,
The lances unlifted, the
trumpet unblown.

VI

And the widows of Ashur are
loud in their wail,
And the idols are broke in the
temple of Baal;
And the might of the Gentile,
unsmote by the sword,
Hath melted like snow in the
glance of the Lord!

A Spirit Pass'd Before Me

FROM *Job*

I

A SPIRIT pass'd before me: I beheld
The face of immortality unveil'd –
Deep sleep came down on every eye save mine –
And there it stood, – all formless – but divine:
Along my bones the creeping flesh did quake;
And as my damp hair stiffen'd, thus it spake:

II

'Is man more just than God? Is man more pure
Than he who deems even Seraphs insecure?
Creatures of clay – vain dwellers in the dust!
The moth survives you, and are ye more just?
Things of a day! you wither ere the night,
Heedless and blind to Wisdom's wasted light!'

Ode to Napoleon Buonaparte

I

'TIS DONE – but yesterday a King!
And arm'd with Kings to strive –
And now thou art a nameless thing:
So abject – yet alive!
Is this the man of thousand thrones,
Who strew'd our earth with hostile bones,
And can he thus survive?
Since he, miscall'd the Morning Star,
Nor man nor fiend hath fallen so far.

II

Ill-minded man! why scourge thy kind
Who bow'd so low the knee?
By gazing on thyself grown blind,
Thou taught'st the rest to see.
With might unquestion'd, – power to save, –
Thine only gift hath been the grave,
To those that worshipp'd thee;
Nor till thy fall could mortals guess
Ambition's less than littleness!

III

Thanks for that lesson – it will teach
To after-warriors more,
Than high Philosophy can preach,
And vainly preach'd before.
That spell upon the minds of men
Breaks never to unite again,
That led them to adore
Those Pagod things of sabre sway,
With fronts of brass, and feet of clay.

IV

The triumph and the vanity,
The rapture of the strife –
The earthquake voice of Victory,
To thee the breath of life;
The sword, the sceptre, and that sway
Which man seem'd made but to obey,
Wherewith renown was rife –
All quelled! – Dark Spirit! what must be
The madness of thy memory!

V

The Desolator desolate!
The Victor overthrown!
The Arbiter of others' fate
A Suppliant for his own!
Is it some yet imperial hope
That with such change can calmly cope?
Or dread of death alone?
To die a prince – or live a slave –
Thy choice is most ignobly brave!

VI

He who of old would rend the oak,
Dream'd not of the rebound:
Chain'd by the trunk he vainly broke –
Alone – how look'd he round?
Thou, in the sternness of thy strength,
An equal deed hast done at length,
And darker fate hast found:
He fell, the forest prowlers' prey;
But thou must eat thy heart away!

VII

The Roman, when his burning heart
Was slaked with blood of Rome,
Threw down the dagger – dared depart,
In savage grandeur, home –
He dared depart in utter scorn
Of men that such a yoke had borne,
Yet left him such a doom!
His only glory was that hour
Of self-upheld abandon'd power.

VIII

The Spaniard, when the lust of sway
Had lost its quickening spell,
Cast crowns for rosaries away,
An empire for a cell;
A strict accountant of his beads,
A subtle disputant on creeds,
His dotage trifled well:
Yet better had he neither known
A bigot's shrine, nor despot's throne.

IX

But thou – from thy reluctant hand
The thunderbolt is wrung –
Too late thou leav'st the high command
To which thy weakness clung;
All Evil Spirit as thou art,
It is enough to grieve the heart
To see thine own unstrung;
To think that God's fair world hath been
The footstool of a thing so mean;

X

And Earth hath spilt her blood for him,
Who thus can hoard his own!
And Monarchs bow'd the trembling limb,
And thank'd him for a throne!
Fair Freedom! we may hold thee dear,
When thus thy mightiest foes their fear
In humblest guise have shown.
Oh! ne'er may tyrant leave behind
A brighter name to lure mankind!

XI

Thine evil deeds are write in gore,
Nor written thus in vain –
Thy triumphs tell of fame no more,
Or deepen every stain:
If thou hadst died as honour dies,
Some new Napoleon might arise,
To shame the world again –
But who would soar the solar height,
To set in such a starless night?

BONAPARTE

XII

Weigh'd in the balance, hero dust
Is vile as vulgar clay;
Thy scales, Mortality! are just
To all that pass away:
But yet methought the living great
Some higher sparks should animate,
To dazzle and dismay:
Nor deem'd Contempt could thus make mirth
Of these, the Conquerors of the earth.

XIII

And she, proud Austria's mournful flower,
Thy still imperial bride;
How bears her breast the torturing hour?
Still clings she to thy side?
Must she too bend, must she too share
Thy late repentance, long despair,
Thou throneless Homicide?
If still she loves thee, hoard that gem, –
'Tis worth thy vanish'd diadem!

XIV

Then haste thee to thy sullen Isle,
And gaze upon the sea;
That element may meet thy smile –
It ne'er was ruled by thee!
Or trace with thine all idle hand
In loitering mood upon the sand
That Earth is now as free!
That Corinth's pedagogue hath now
Transferr'd his by-word to thy brow.

XV

Thou Timour! in his captive's cage
What thoughts will there be thine,
While brooding in thy prison'd rage?
But one – 'The world was mine!'
Unless, like he of Babylon,
All sense is with thy sceptre gone,
Life will not long confine
That spirit pour'd so widely forth –
So long obey'd – so little worth!

XVI

Or, like the thief of fire from heaven,
Wilt thou withstand the shock?
And share with him, the unforgiven,
His vulture and his rock!
Foredoom'd by God – by man accurst,
And that last act, though not thy worst,
The very Fiend's arch mock;
He in his fall preserved his pride,
And, if a mortal, had as proudly died!

XVII

There was a day – there was an hour,
While earth was Gaul's – Gaul thine –
When that immeasurable power
Unsated to resign
Had been an act of purer fame
Than gathers round Marengo's name
And gilded thy decline,
Through the long twilight of all time,
Despite some passing clouds of crime.

XVIII

But thou forsooth must be a king
And don the purple vest,
As if that foolish robe could wring
Remembrance from thy breast.
Where is that faded garment? where
The gewgaws thou wert fond to wear,
The star, the string, the crest?
Vain froward child of empire! say,
Are all thy playthings snatched away?

XIX

Where may the wearied eye repose
When gazing on the Great;
Where neither guilty glory glows,
Nor despicable state?
Yes – one – the first – the last – the best –
The Cincinnatus of the West,
Whom envy dared not hate,
Bequeath'd the name of Washington,
To make man blush there was but one!

Stanzas to Augusta

I

THOUGH THE day of my destiny's over,
And the star of my fate hath declined,
Thy soft heart refused to discover
The faults which so many could find;
Though thy soul with my grief was acquainted,
It shrunk not to share it with me,
And the love which my spirit hath painted
It never hath found but in *thee*.

II

Then when nature around me is smiling,
The last smile which answers to mine,
I do not believe it beguiling,
Because it reminds me of thine;
And when winds are at war with the ocean,
As the breasts I believed in with me,
If their billows excite an emotion,
It is that they bear me from *thee*.

III

Though the rock of my last hope is shiver'd,
And its fragments are sunk in the wave,
Though I feel that my soul is deliver'd
To pain – it shall not be its slave.
There is many a pang to pursue me:
They may crush, but they shall not contemn;
They may torture, but shall not subdue me;
'Tis of *thee* that I think – not of them.

IV

Though human, thou didst not deceive me,
Though woman, thou didst not forsake,
Though loved, thou forborest to grieve me,
Though slander'd, thou never couldst shake;
Though trusted, thou didst not disclaim me;
Though parted, it was not to fly;
Though watchful, 'twas not to defame me,
Nor, mute, that the world might belie.

V

Yet I blame not the world, nor despise it,
Nor the war of the many with one;
If my soul was not fitted to prize it,
'Twas folly not sooner to shun:
And if dearly that error hath cost me,
And more than I once could foresee,
I have found that, whatever it lost me,
It could not deprive me of *thee*.

VI

From the wreck of the past, which hath perish'd,
Thus much I at least may recall,
It hath taught me that what I most cherish'd
Deserved to be dearest of all:
In the desert a fountain is springing,
In the wide waste there still is a tree,
And a bird in the solitude singing,
Which speaks to my spirit of *thee*.

English Bards and Scotch Reviewers

EXTRACT

BEHOLD! IN various throngs the scribbling crew,
For notice eager, pass in long review:
Each spurs his jaded Pegasus apace,
And rhyme and blank maintain an equal race;
Sonnets on sonnets crowd, and ode on ode;
And tales of terror jostle on the road;
Immeasurable measures move along;
For simpering folly loves a varied song,
To strange mysterious dulness still the friend,
Admires the strain she cannot comprehend.
Thus Lays of Minstrels – may they be the last! –
On half-strung harps whine mournful to the blast.
While mountain spirits prate to river sprites,
That dames may listen to the sound at nights;
And goblin brats, of Gilpin Horner's brood,
Decoy young border-nobles through the wood,
And skip at every step, Lord knows how high,
And frighten foolish babes, the Lord knows why;
While high-born ladies in their magic cell,
Forbidding knights to read who cannot spell,
Despatch a courier to a wizard's grave,
And fight with honest men to shield a knave.

Johannes Milton.
1671

Next view in state, proud prancing on his roan,
The golden-crested haughty Marmion,
Now forging scrolls, now foremost in the fight,
Not quite a felon, yet but half a knight,
The gibbet or the field prepared to grace;
A mighty mixture of the great and base.
And think'st thou, Scott! by vain conceit perchance,
On public taste to foist thy stale romance,
Though Murray with his Miller may combine
To yield thy muse just half-a-crown per line?
No! when the sons of song descend to trade,
Their bays are sear, their former laurels fade.
Let such forego the poet's sacred name,
Who rack their brains for lucre, not for fame:
Still for stern Mammon may they toil in vain!
And sadly gaze on gold they cannot gain!
Such be their meed, such still the just reward
Of prostituted muse and hireling bard!
For this we spurn Apollo's venal son,
And bid a long 'good night to Marmion.'

These are the themes that claim our plaudits now;
These are the bards to whom the muse must bow;
While Milton, Dryden, Pope, alike forgot,
Resign their hallow'd bays to Walter Scott. . .

Next comes the dull disciple of thy school,
That mild apostate from poetic rule,
The simple Wordsworth, framer of a lay
As soft as evening in his favourite May,
Who warns his friend 'to shake off toil and trouble,
And quit his books, for fear of growing double;'
Who, both by precept and example, shows
That prose is verse, and verse is merely prose;
Convincing all, by demonstration plain,
Poetic souls delight in prose insane;
And Christmas stories tortured into rhyme
Contain the essence of the true sublime.
Thus, when he tells the tale of Betty Foy,
The idiot mother of 'an idiot boy';
A moon-struck, silly lad, who lost his way,
And, like his bard, confounded night with day;
So close on each pathetic part he dwells,
And each adventure so sublimely tells,
That all who view the 'idiot in his glory'
Conceive the bard the hero of the story.

Shall gentle Coleridge pass unnoticed here,
To turgid ode and tumid stanza dear?
Though themes of innocence amuse him best,
Yet still obscurity's a welcome guest.
If Inspiration should her aid refuse
To him who takes a pixy for a muse,
Yet none in lofty numbers can surpass
The bard who soars to elegise an ass.
So well the subject suits his noble mind,
He brays the laureat of the long-ear'd kind.

Sonnet to Lake Leman

ROUSSEAU – VOLTAIRE – our Gibbon – and De Staël –
Leman! these names are worthy of thy shore,
Thy shore of names like these! wert thou no more
Their memory thy remembrance would recall:
To them thy banks were lovely as to all,
But they have made them lovelier, for the lore
Of mighty minds doth hallow in the core
Of human hearts the ruin of a wall
Where dwelt the wise and wondrous; but by thee
How much more, Lake of Beauty! do we feel,
In sweetly gliding o'er thy crystal sea,
The wild glow of that no ungentle zeal,
Which the heirs of immortality
Is proud, and makes the breath of glory real!

Childe Harold's Pilgrimage

CANTO I

EXTRACT

I

OH, THOU! in Hellas deem'd of heavenly birth,
Muse! form'd or fabled at the minstrel's will!
Since shamed full oft by later lyres on earth,
Mine dares not call thee from thy sacred hill:
Yet there I've wander'd by thy vaunted rill;
Yes! sighed o'er Delphi's long deserted shrine,
Where, save that feeble fountain, all is still;
Nor mote my shell awake the weary Nine
To grace so plain a tale – this lowly lay of mine.

II

Whilome in Albion's isle there dwelt a youth,
Who ne in virtue's ways did take delight;
But spent his days in riot most uncouth,
And vex'd with mirth the drowsy ear of Night.
Ah, me! in sooth he was a shameless wight,
Sore given to revel and ungodly glee;
Few earthly things found favour in his sight
Save concubines and carnal companie,
And flaunting wassailers of high and low degree.

III

Childe Harold was he hight: – but whence his name
And lineage long, it suits me not to say;
Suffice it, that perchance they were of fame,
And had been glorious in another day:
But one sad losel soils a name for aye,
However mighty in the olden time;
Nor all that heralds rake from coffin'd clay,
Nor florid prose, nor honied lies of rhyme,
Can blazon evil deeds, or consecrate a crime.

IV

Childe Harold bask'd him in the noontide sun,
Disporting there like any other fly;
Nor deem'd before his little day was done
One blast might chill him into misery.
But long ere scarce a third of his pass'd by,
Worse than adversity the Childe befell;
He felt the fulness of satiety:
Then loathed he in his native land to dwell,
Which seemed to him more lone than Eremite's sad cell.

V

For he through Sin's long labyrinth had run,
Nor made atonement when he did amiss,
Had sigh'd to many though he loved but one,
And that loved one, alas! could ne'er be his.
Ah, happy she! to 'scape from him whose kiss
Had been pollution unto aught so chaste;
Who soon had left her charms for vulgar bliss,
And spoil'd her goodly lands to gild his waste,
Nor calm domestic peace had ever deign'd to taste.

VI

And now Childe Harold was sore sick at heart,
And from his fellow bacchanals would flee;
'Tis said, at times the sullen tear would start,
But pride congealed the drop within his ee:
Apart he stalk'd in joyless reverie,
And from his native land resolved to go,
And visit scorching climes beyond the sea;
With pleasure drugg'd, he almost long'd for woe,
And e'en for change of scene would seek the shades below.

VII

The Childe departed from his father's hall:
It was a vast and venerable pile;
So old, it seemèd only not to fall,
Yet strength was pillar'd in each massy aisle.
Monastic dome! condemn'd to uses vile!
Where Superstition once had made her den
Now Paphian girls were known to sing and smile;
And monks might deem their time was come agen,
If ancient tales say true, nor wrong these holy men.

VIII

Yet oft-times in his maddest mirthful mood
Strange pangs would flash along Childe Harold's brow,
As if the memory of some deadly feud
Or disappointed passion lurked below:
But this none knew, nor haply cared to know;
For his was not that open, artless soul
That feels relief by bidding sorrow flow,
Nor sought he friend to counsel or condole,
Whate'er this grief mote be, which he could not control.

IX

And none did love him: though to hall and bower
He gather'd revellers from far and near
He knew them flatt'rers of the festal hour;
The heartless parasites of present cheer.
Yea! none did love him – not his lemans dear –
But pomp and power alone are woman's care,
And where these are light Eros finds a feere;
Maidens, like moths, are ever caught by glare,
And Mammon wins his way where Seraphs might despair.

X

Childe Harold had a mother – not forgot,
Though parting from that mother he did shun;
A sister whom he loved, but saw her not
Before his weary pilgrimage begun:
If friends he had, he bade adieu to none.
Yet deem not thence his breast a breast of steel:
Ye, who have known what 'tis to dote upon
A few dear objects, will in sadness feel
Such partings break the heart they fondly hope to heal.

XI

His house, his home, his heritage, his lands,
The laughing dames in whom he did delight,
Whose large blue eyes, fair locks, and snowy hands,
Might shake the saintship of an anchorite,
And long had fed his youthful appetite;
His goblets brimm'd with every costly wine,
And all that mote to luxury invite,
Without a sigh he left, to cross the brine,
And traverse Paynim shores, and pass Earth's central line.

XII

The sails were fill'd, and fair the light winds blew,
As glad to waft him from his native home;
And fast the white rocks faded from his view,
And soon were lost in circumambient foam:
And then, it may be, of his wish to roam
Repented he, but in his bosom slept
The silent thought, nor from his lips did come
One word of wail, whilst others sate and wept,
And to the reckless gales unmanly moaning kept.

CANTO IV

EXTRACT

CXXI

Oh Love! no habitant of earth thou art –
An unseen seraph, we believe in thee, –
A faith whose martyrs are the broken heart, –
But never yet hath seen, nor e'er shall see
The naked eye, thy form, as it should be;
The mind hath made thee, as it peopled heaven,
Even with its own desiring phantasy,
And to a thought such shape and image given,
As haunts the unquench'd soul – parch'd, wearied, wrung, and riven.

CXXII

Of its own beauty is the mind diseased,
And fevers into false creation: – where,
Where are the forms the sculptor's soul hath seiz'd?
In him alone. Can Nature show so fair?
Where are the charms and virtues which we dare
Conceive in boyhood and pursue as men,
The unreach'd Paradise of our despair,
Which o'er-informs the pencil and the pen,
And overpowers the page where it would bloom again?

CXXIII

Who loves, raves – 'tis youth's frenzy – but the cure
Is bitterer still, as charm by charm unwinds
Which robed our idols, and we see too sure
Nor worth nor beauty dwells from out the mind's
Ideal shape of such; yet still it binds
The fatal spell, and still it draws us on,
Reaping the whirlwind from the oft-sown winds;
The stubborn heart, its alchemy begun,
Seems ever near the prize – wealthiest when most undone.

CXXIV

We wither from our youth, we gasp away –
Sick – sick; unfound the boon, unslaked the thirst,
Though to the last, in verge of our decay,
Some phantom lures, such as we sought at first –
But all too late, – so are we doubly curst.
Love, fame, ambition, avarice – 'tis the same,
Each idle, and all ill, and none the worst –
For all are meteors with a different name,
And Death the sable smoke where vanishes the flame.

CXXV

Few – none – find what they love or could have loved,
Though accident, blind contact, and the strong
Necessity of loving, have removed
Antipathies – but to recur, ere long,
Envenom'd with irrevocable wrong;
And Circumstance, that unspiritual god
And miscreator, makes and helps along
Our coming evils with a crutch-like rod,
Whose touch turns Hope to dust, – the dust we all have trod.

CXXVI

Our life is a false nature: 'tis not in
The harmony of things, – this hard decree,
This uneradicable taint of sin,
This boundless upas, this all-blasting tree,
Whose root is earth, whose leaves and branches be
The skies which rain their plagues on men like dew –
Disease, death, bondage – all the woes we see,
And worse, the woes we see not – which throb through
The immediacable soul, with heart-aches ever new.

CXXVII

Yet let us ponder boldly – 'tis a base
Abandonment of reason to resign
Our right of thought – our last and only place
Of refuge; this, at least, shall still be mine:
Though from our birth the faculty divine
Is chain'd and tortured – cabin'd, cribb'd, confined,
And bred in darkness, lest the truth should shine
Too brightly on the unpreparèd mind,
The beam pours in, for time and skill will couch the blind.

CXXVIII

Arches on arches! as it were that Rome,
Collecting the chief trophies of her line,
Would build up all her triumphs in one dome,
Her Coliseum stands; the moonbeams shine
As 'twere its natural torches, for divine
Should be the light which streams here to illume
This long-explored but still exhaustless mine
Of contemplation; and the azure gloom
Of an Italian night, where the deep skies assume

CXXIX

Hues which have words, and speak to ye of heaven,
Floats o'er this vast and wondrous monument,
And shadows forth its glory. There is given
Unto the things of earth, which Time hath bent,
A spirit's feeling, and where he hath leant
His hand, but broke his scythe, there is a power
And magic in the ruin'd battlement,
For which the palace of the present hour
Must yield its pomp, and wait till ages are its dower.

CXXX

Oh Time! the beautifier of the dead,
Adorner of the ruin, comforter
And only healer when the heart hath bled;
Time! the corrector where our judgments err,
The test of truth, love – sole philosopher,
For all beside are sophists – from thy thrift,
Which never loses though it doth defer –
Time the avenger! unto thee I lift
My hands, and eyes, and heart, and crave of thee a gift:

CXXXI

Amidst this wreck, where thou hast made a shrine
And temple more divinely desolate,
Among thy mightier offerings here are mine,
Ruins of years, though few, yet full of fate:
If thou hast ever seen me too elate,
Hear not me; but if calmly I have borne
Good, and reserved my pride against the hate
Which shall not whelm me, let me not have worn
This iron in my soul in vain – shall *they* not mourn?

Don Juan

CANTO I

—— EXTRACT ——

CXXII

... 'Tis sweet to hear
At midnight on the blue and moonlit deep
The song and oar of Adria's gondolier,
By distance mellow'd, o'er the waters sweep;
'Tis sweet to see the evening star appear;
'Tis sweet to listen as the night-winds creep
From leaf to leaf; 'tis sweet to view on high
The rainbow, based on ocean, span the sky.

CXXIII

'Tis sweet to hear the watch-dog's honest bark
Bay deep-mouth'd welcome as we draw near home;
'Tis sweet to know there is an eye will mark
Our coming, and look brighter when we come;
'Tis sweet to be awaken'd by the lark
Or lull'd by falling waters; sweet the hum
Of bees, the voice of girls, the song of birds,
The lisp of children, and their earliest words.

CXXIV

Sweet is the vintage, when the showering grapes
In Bacchanal profusion reel to earth,
Purple and gushing: sweet are our escapes
From civic revelry to rural mirth;
Sweet to the miser are his glittering heaps,
Sweet to the father is his first-born's birth,
Sweet is revenge – especially to women,
Pillage to soldiers, prize-money to seamen.

CXXV

Sweet is a legacy, and passing sweet
The unexpected death of some old lady
Or gentleman of seventy years complete,
Who've made 'us youth' wait too – too long already
For an estate, or cash, or country seat,
Still breaking, but with stamina so steady
That all the Israelites are fit to mob its
Next owner for their double-damn'd post-obits.

CXXVI

'Tis sweet to win, no matter how, one's laurels,
By blood or ink;'tis sweet to put an end
To strife: 'tis sometimes sweet to have our quarrels
Particularly with a tiresome friend:
Sweet is old wine in bottles, ale in barrels;
Dear is the helpless creature we defend
Against the world; and dear the schoolboy spot
We ne'er forget, though there we are forgot.

CXXVII

But sweeter still than this, than these, than all,
Is first and passionate love – it stands alone,
Like Adam's recollection of his fall;
The tree of knowledge has been pluck'd – all's known –
And life yields nothing further to recall
Worthy of this ambrosial sin, so shown,
No doubt in fable, as the unforgiven
Fire which Prometheus filch'd for us from heaven.

CXXVIII

Man's a strange animal, and makes strange use
Of his own nature, and the various arts,
And likes particularly to produce
Some new experiment to show his parts;
This is the age of oddities let loose,
Where different talents find their different marts;
You'd best begin with truth, and when you've lost your
Labour, there's a sure market for imposture.

CXXIX

What opposite discoveries we have seen!
(Signs of true genius, and of empty pockets.)
One makes new noses, one a guillotine,
One breaks your bones, one sets them in their sockets;
But vaccination certainly has been
A kind antithesis to Congreve's rockets,
With which the Doctor paid off an old pox,
By borrowing a new one from an ox.

CXXX

Bread has been made (indifferent) from potatoes;
And galvanism has set some corpses grinning,
But has not answer'd like the apparatus
Of the Humane Society's beginning,
By which men are unsuffocated gratis:
What wondrous new machines have late been spinning!
I said the small pox has gone out of late;
Perhaps it may be follow'd by the great.

CXXXI

'Tis said the great came from America;
Perhaps it may set out on its return, –
The population there so spreads, they say
'Tis grown high time to thin it in its turn,
With war, or plague, or famine, any way,
So that civilisation they may learn;
And which in ravage the more loathsome evil is –
Their real lues, or our pseudo-syphilis?

CXXXII

This is the patent age of new inventions
For killing bodies, and for saving souls,
All propagated with the best intentions;
Sir Humphry Davy's lantern, by which coals
Are safely mined for in the mode he mentions,
Tombuctoo travels, voyages to the Poles,
Are ways to benefit mankind, as true,
Perhaps, as shooting them at Waterloo.

CXXXIII

Man's a phenomenon, one knows not what,
And wonderful beyond all wondrous measure;
'Tis pity though, in this sublime world, that
Pleasure's a sin, and sometimes sin's a pleasure;
Few mortals know what end they would be at,
But whether glory, power, or love, or treasure,
The path is through perplexing ways, and when
The goal is gain'd, we die, you know – and then –

Prometheus

I

TITAN! TO whose immortal eyes
The sufferings of mortality,
Seen in their sad reality,
Were not as things that gods despise;
What was thy pity's recompense?
A silent suffering, and intense;
The rock, the vulture, and the chain,
All that the proud can feel of pain,
The agony they do not show,
The suffocating sense of woe,
Which speaks but in its loneliness,
And then is jealous lest the sky
Should have a listener, nor will sigh
Until its voice is echoless.

II

Titan! to thee the strife was given
Between the suffering and the will,
Which torture where they cannot kill;
And the inexorable Heaven,
And the deaf tyranny of Fate,
The ruling principle of Hate,
Which for its pleasure doth create
The things it may annihilate,
Refused thee even the boon to die:
The wretched gift eternity
Was thing – and thou hast borne it well.
All that the Thunderer wrung from thee
Was but the menace which flung back on him the
torments of thy rack;
The fate thou didst so well foresee,
But would not to appease him tell;

And in thy Silence was his Sentence,
And in his Soul a vain repentance,
And evil dread so ill dissembled,
That in his hand the lightnings trembled.

III

Thy Godlike crime was to be kind,
To render with thy precepts less
The sum of human wretchedness,
And strengthen Man with his own mind;
But baffled as thou wert from high,
Still in thy patient energy,
In the endurance, and repulse
Of thine impenetrable Spirit,
Which Earth and Heaven could not convulse,
A mighty lesson we inherit:
Thou art a symbol and a sign
To Mortals of their fate and force;
Like thee, Man is in part divine,
A troubled stream from a pure source;
And Man in portions can foresee
His own funereal destiny;
His wretchedness and his resistance,
And his sad unallied existence:
To which his Spirit may oppose
Itself – and equal to all woes,
And a firm will, and a deep sense,
Which even in torture can descry
Its own concenter'd recompense,
Triumphant where it dares defy,
And making Death a Victory.

From *Stanzas*

WHEN A man hath no freedom to fight for at home,
Let him combat for that of his neighbours;
Let him think of the glories of Greece and of Rome,
And get knock'd on the head for his labours.
To do good to mankind is the chivalrous plan,
And is always as nobly requited;
Then battle for freedom wherever you can,
And, if not shot or hang'd you'll get knighted.

Lines on Hearing that Lady Byron Was Ill

AND THOU wert sad – yet I was not with thee;
And thou wert sick, and yet I was not near;
Methought that joy and health alone could be
Where I was not – and pain and sorrow here!
And is it thus? – it is as I foretold,
And shall be more so; for the mind recoils
Upon itself, and the wreck'd heart lies cold,
While heaviness collects the shatter'd spoils.
It is not in the storm nor in the strife
We feel benumb'd, and wish to be no more,
But in the after-silence on the shore,
When all is lost, except a little life.
I am too well avenged! – but 'twas my right:
Whate'er my sins might be, thou wert not sent
To be the Nemesis who should requite –
Nor did Heaven choose so near an instrument.
Mercy is for the merciful! – if thou
Had been of such, 'twill be accorded now.
Thy nights are banish'd from the realms of sleep! –
Yes! they may flatter thee, but thou shalt feel
A hollow agony which will not heal,
For thou art pillow'd on a curse too deep;
Thou hast sown in my sorrow, and must reap
The bitter harvest in a woe as real!
I have had many foes, but none like thee;
For 'gainst the rest myself I could defend,
And be avenged, or turn them into friend;
But thou in safe implacability
Hadst nought to dread – in thy own weakness shielded,

And in my love, which hath but too much yielded,
And spared, for thy sake, some I should not spare;
And thus upon the world – trust in thy truth,
And the wild fame of my ungovern'd youth –
On things that were not, and on things that are –
Even upon such a basis hast thou built
A monument, whose cement hath been guilt!
The moral Clytemnestra of thy lord,
And hew'd down, with an unsuspected sword,
Fame, peace, and hope – and all the better life,
Which, but for this cold treason of thy heart,
Might still have risen from out the grave of strife,
And found a nobler duty than to part.
But of thy virtues didst thou make a vice,
Trafficking with them in a purpose cold,
For present anger, and for future gold –
And buying others' grief at any price.
And thus once enter'd into crooked ways,
The earthly truth, which was thy proper praise,
Did not still walk beside thee – but at times,
And with a breast unknowing its own crimes,
Deceit, averments incompatible,
Equivocations, and the thoughts which dwell
In Janus-spirits – the significant eye
Which learns to lie with silence – the pretext
Of prudence, with advantages annex'd –
The acquiescence in all things which tend,
No matter how, to the desired end –
All found a place in thy philosophy.
The means were worthy, and the end is won –
I would not do by thee as thou hast done!

The Chain I Gave
FROM THE TURKISH

THE CHAIN I gave was fair to view
The lute I added sweet in sound;
The heart that offered both was true,
And ill deserved the fate it found.

These gifts were charm'd by secret spell,
Thy truth in absence to divine
And they have done their duty well,–
Alas! they could not teach thee thine.

That chain was firm in every link,
But not to bear a stranger's touch;
That lute was sweet – till thou could'st think
In other hands its notes were such.

Let him who from thy neck unbound
The chain which shiver'd in his grasp
Who saw that lute refuse to sound,
Restring the chords, renew the clasp.

When thou wert changed, they alter'd too;
The chain is broke, the music mute.
'Tis past – to them and thee adieu –
False heart, frail chain, and silent lute.

On Finding a Fan

IN ONE who felt as once he felt,
This might, perhaps, have fann'd the flame;
But now his heart no more will melt,
Because that heart is not the same.

As when the ebbing flames are low,
The aid which once improved their light,
And bade them burn with fiercer glow,
Now quenches all their blaze in night.

Thus has it been with passion's fires –
As many a boy and girl remembers –
While every hope of love expires,
Extinguish'd with thy dying embers.

The first, though not a spark survive,
Some careful hand may teach to burn;
The last, alas! can ne'er survive;
No touch can bid its warmth return

Or, if it chance to wake again,
Not always doom'd its heat to smother,
It sheds (so wayward fates ordain)
Its former warmth around another.

Sonnet on Chillon

ETERNAL SPIRIT of the chainless Mind!
Brightest in dungeons, Liberty! thou art,
For there thy habitation is the heart –
The heart which love of thee alone can bind;
And when thy sons to fetters are consign'd –
To fetters, and the damp vault's dayless gloom,
Their country conquers with their martyrdom,
And Freedom's fame finds wings on every wind.
Chillon! thy prison is a holy place,
And thy sad floor an altar – for 'twas trod,
Until his very steps have left a trace
Worn, as if thy cold pavement were a sod,
By Bonnivard! – May none those marks efface!
For they appeal from tyranny to God.

Index to First Lines

Notes on Illustrations

3 Lord Byron after a portrait painted by Thomas Phillips, by William Essex (Stapleton Collection). Courtesy of the Bridgeman Art Library.

5 *Venice, the Piazzetta with the Ceremony of the Doge* by Turner (Tate Gallery, London). Courtesy of Visual Arts Library.

7 *Portrait of Byron* by English School (The Fine Art Society, London). Courtesy of The Bridgeman Art Library.

13 *Lord Byron, shaking the dust of England from his shoes,* from 'The Poets Corner' by Max Beerbohm, published. by William Heinemann. Courtesy of The Bridgeman Art Library.

14-15 *A View of the Lake and Ruins of the Abbey at Painshill, Surrey* by G. Barrett and S. Gilpin (Roy Miles Gallery, London). Courtesy of The Bridgeman Art Library.

21 *The Young Lovers* by Gerard Hoet (Haynes Fine Art at The Bindery Galleries). Courtesy of The Bridgeman Art Library.

24 *A Greek Ode* by Alfred W. Elmore (Roy Miles Gallery, London). Courtesy of The Bridgeman Art Library.

28 *The Lament* by Sir Edward Burne-Jones (William Morris Gallery, Walthamstow). Courtesy of The Bridgeman Art Library.

32 *Ophelia* by Paul Albert Steck (Musée du Petit Palais, Paris). Courtesy of Giraudon and The Bridgeman Art Library.

34 *Sweet Sounds* by John William Godward (Roy Miles Gallery, London). Courtesy of The Bridgeman Art Library.

37 Detail from *Lord Byron, shaking the dust of England from his shoes,* from 'The Poets Corner' by Max Beerbohm, published. by William Heinemann. Courtesy of The Bridgeman Art Library.

38-9 *Pilgrims approaching Jerusalem* by David Roberts (Royal Holloway & Bedford New College, Surrey). Courtesy of The Bridgeman Art Library.

43 *Lord Byron reposing in the House of a Fisherman having swum the Hellespont* by Sir William Allan (Roy Miles, London). Courtesy of The Bridgeman Art Library.

48 *Inspiration of Caedmon* by Lexden L. Pocock (Cheltenham Art Gallery & Museums, Glos.). Courtesy of The Bridgeman Art Library.

50-1 *Battle of Waterloo* by Joseph William Allen (Apsley House, London). Courtesy of The Bridgeman Art Library.

55 *Bonaparte crossing the Alps* by Jacques Louis David (Chateau De Malmaison, Paris). Courtesy of The Bridgeman Art Library.

58 *The Coronation of Napoleon I* by Jean-Auguste Dominique Ingres (Musée De L'Armee, Paris). Courtesy of The Bridgeman Art Library.

60 *Augusta Leigh, Byron's Sister* by Anonymous (Christie's, London). Courtesy of The Bridgeman Art Library.

63 Detail from *A Four Leaf Screen with Portraits of Shakespeare, Milton, Chaucer and Spenser* by William Bell Scott (Christie's, London). Courtesy of The Bridgeman Art Library.

66-7 *Castle of Chillon* by Phillippe de Louthebourg (Cheltenham Art Gallery & Museums, Gloucestershire). Courtesy of The Bridgeman Art Library.

71-5 Detail from *The Bright Stone of Honour (Ehrenbreitstein) and the Tomb of Marceau, from Byron's 'Childe Harold'* by Joseph Mallord William Turner (Private Collection). Courtesy of The Bridgeman Art Library.

75 Detail from *The Bright Stone of Honour (Ehrenbreitstein) and the Tomb of Marceau, from Byron's 'Childe Harold'* by Joseph Mallord William Turner (Private Collection). Courtesy of The Bridgeman Art Library.

78-9 *Byron Laments* by William James Muller (The Fine Art Society, London). Courtesy of The Bridgeman Art Library.

85 *The Torture of Prometheus* by Jean-Louis-Cesar Lair (Musée Crozatier, Le Puy en Velay, France). Courtesy of The Bridgeman Art Library.

89 *In Memorian* by Evelyn de Morgan (The De Morgan Foundation, London). Courtesy of The Bridgeman Art Library.

93 *Nerissa* by John William Godward (Private Collection). Courtesy of The Bridgeman Art Library.

94 *The Prisoner of Chillon* by Ford Madox Brown (Manchester City Art Galleries). Courtesy of The Bridgeman Art Library.